W0082337

The Groundnote

The Groundnote

poems by Janet Kaplan

Janet Kaplan

Susan —
for the honor
of reading with
you tonight

♡, Janet
6/2000
NYC

ALICE JAMES BOOKS
Farmington, Maine

Copyright © 1998 by Janet Kaplan
All rights reserved
Printed in the United States of America

Library of Congress Cataloging-in-Publication Data
Kaplan, Janet, 1958-
        The Groundnote: poems / by Janet Kaplan.
        p. cm.
        ISBN 1-882295-19-6 : $11.95 paperback
        I. Title.
PS3561.A5592G7   1998
811'.54–dc21   98-4905 CIP

Book design by Russell Gordon

Three lines from "Kaddish" from *Collected Poems 1947-1980* by
Allen Ginsberg. Copyright © 1959 by Allen Ginsberg. Copyright
renewed. Reprinted by permission of HarperCollins Publishers, Inc.

Alice James Books gratefully acknowledges support from
the University of Maine at Farmington
and the National Endowment for the Arts.

Alice James Books are published by the Alice James Poetry Cooperative, Inc.,
an affiliate of the University of Maine at Farmington.
Alice James Books
98 Main Street
Farmington, Maine 04938

I dedicate this book to my father.

Acknowledgments

A number of poems in this collection first appeared, in earlier versions, or are forthcoming in the following periodicals:
Alaska Quarterly Review, American Literary Review, Crone's Nest, Global City Review, The Greensboro Review, Ms., The Massachusetts Review, The Paris Review, Response, Sarah Lawrence Review, and *Western Humanities Review.*

Several poems also appeared in the chapbook *The Solid Ground,* published by the Premier Poets Chapbook Series, Rhode Island (with gratitude to its editor, Michele Cooper).

I wish to thank the Bronx Council on the Arts for the BRIO award (an individual artist's grant); and the Corporation of Yaddo, the Ragdale Foundation, the Virginia Center for the Creative Arts, and the Vermont Studio Center for residencies during which much of this book was written and completed. Thanks go to my father for his fundamental support, way beyond the call of reason. My deep gratitude to my Sarah Lawrence teachers, and to Craig Gordon, Russell Gordon, Richard Howard, Alison W. Koffler, Molly Peacock (otherwise the slumber might have lasted even longer, the voicelessness), Beth Pearson, Jonathan Emanuel Shapiro, and Judith Taylor, and to the Alice James Books collective, especially Ellen Doré Watson, Adrienne Su, Peg Peoples, and Sharon Kraus: generous teachers all.

For the memory of my mother.
Sometimes it's real and sometimes it isn't.

For Craig, my own beast.

Contents

Chansons   *11*

One

Fourteen   *15*
Poem   *17*
The New Age   *20*
    1: Sex Kitten
    2: Attachments
    3: Burnt Orange Taxi
    4: Blue Lights
    5: The Little Prophesies
    6: Rough Neighborhood
Unfinished Music   *26*
Writer   *31*
The Reconciler   *36*
Lucifer of the Mind   *38*
Pibloktoq   *39*

Two

Ziusudra in Warsaw   *43*
Storm Windows: Broken Song   *45*
The Living Man   *48*
To My Mother's Parents   *50*
Wildfire   *52*
Cradle, Keel   *54*

Three

The Sirens   *59*
This City   *62*
Monster   *64*
Sister   *66*
After the Sacrifice   *67*
The Bridge of Sighs   *68*
Answer   *72*
Pelham Bay   *74*

Notes   *77*
About the Author   *79*

"—yet Triumph,
to have been here, and changed, like a tree, broken, or flower—
fed to the ground—but mad"
—ALLEN GINSBERG, "Kaddish"

The Groundnote

Chansons

The world's first *chanson de geste:* Inanna of Heaven
descending to her sister, the grief-stricken

widow of Hell. In darkness who's totally pleased
to see another's allotment of light?

Queen Ereshkigal turns Inanna
into a hunk of rotting meat and hangs her

from a peg on the wall. This Sumerian
feud—sister evil, sister good—recurs

again, and again in occupied France:
A glistery singer of love (born to

the gutters of Paris) takes a name, Piaf,
and by night descends the coils and labyrinths

of smoke-dimmed cabarets. *Nothing,* she sings.
I regret nothing. What does the famous

singer want? To forget where, blind and abandoned,
she came from. Then Wisdom sends two specks of dirt

from beneath its fingernails to rescue
Inanna. The dirt moans and groans, and so

befriends Queen Ereshkigal. Piaf's
night-world audience—bone-tired soldiers,

war widows—nod their heads, wipe tears. *Who are you?*
they ask (as Ereshkigal asks). *Moaning-*

groaning-sighing with us? If you're a god
we'll bless you. If you're mortal, we'll

give you a gift. But Piaf doesn't want
what anyone offers. *I want only*

that corpse, she says, pointing where she had stood.
The corpse that belongs to me. Ereshkigal

returns Inanna to the living world.
Those who love Piaf hold her head above

the porcelain as she vomits alcohol
and blood. They admit her to drying-out

hospitals. They forgive her harsh words,
her unwashed hair. *Life is so rosy*, she sings

—trying still to forget the groundnote—
every night until her death. *So rosy*,

echo the emissaries of dirt, who know
to make one and the same song

of Heaven and Hell.

One

"A woman will be heard softly singing and accompanying herself by striking the fist of one hand with the palm of the second.... The rhythm and motion continue for some time, during which she usually tears off her clothing, and ends in a fit of crying or screaming in which she may imitate the cry of some familiar animal or bird."

—A. A. Brill, "Pibloktoq or Hysteria Among Peary's Eskimos," 1913

Fourteen

When the woman asleep on the school-yard bench
is your mother, you can't ignore
the jump-start in your stomach, can't let the image
flicker and fade like a poor picture on TV,
can't shut the scene of her torn skirt, her legs

absently spread to a show of her sex,
the copper hairs glowing like electric wires
down her white thighs, can't yank the cord
plugging your life to her body, no,
you stay tuned to the crusts of breakfast

glazed down her chin like leftovers
on a snack-tray no one could bother to wipe,
there is no interruption as you stare
rapt as any lecher at the frayed checkered shirt
barely buttoning her chest, the life in her

clearly rising, her breathing effortless and constant
as the road runner beeping up and down
the cartoon hills while the lunatic coyote
sets the detonator over
and over, but you can't stop

that crime, you choke yourself
on tears, you keep your hands to yourself
though you want to throw a cloak, thick and warm
with your love, over her half-naked body,
this is all you want, to protect her,

hide her from the audience, the throng
that comes for the spectacle, you want to steal her
from those who do not love her as, truly,
you do, you who know by heart this madwoman
who does not stay in the attic

but comes to greet you in real life, exposing
your real life at the place where somehow you must
show up every day to study your lines,
where somehow you must perform
this dress rehearsal of yourself—

Poem

From New York's outer boroughs toward center,
Central Park and the cymbalistic climax
to the 1812 Overture—and, over
Manhattan's half-moon, the accompanying
explosions (cyclamen, sunflower,
chrysanthemum) flaring into blossom.

Such hue and cry for a midsummer's night!
What magician could concoct a sleep,
let alone a dream of love, among
the humid patchwork of family
picnic blankets, chicken sandwiches, loose-
corked wine fit, perhaps, to wash down Bottom's

good dry oats? Here's no place for miracles
or finery of taste: at one blanket,
the scent of banana and Pampers;
at another, a nastier mix, suburban-
fresh, of Aramis and Eau de Love. And there,
so close to the first violins that they

can see the limbered sweated necks, two
whose debt to one another resembles
nothing less than limited war.
The coupling, way beyond flammable,
beyond spark. A kinetic sort of rage
but deep in the bone, where it acts to numb

the limbs, the heart. A settlement, of sorts,
which might explain so strong a lust
for Tchaikovsky's overdose of peaks.
And with them their beaded child, duly
polyestered in halter blouse and cut-off
dungarees. Impossibly, her hair's neatened,

even in the humid heat, to a melanite
sheen. "I'm sitting somewhere else," she,
the seventeen-year-old, says to those two, those
sullen melded knots of ma and dad. No
response, so into the crowd with her then.
A weak stomach-clenching girl, whose worst fear

is her future, that miasma of hazards
—and if *future* might be synonymic
of *now*, she is not a customer.
Inside, the girl-soul is not available
for her mind's use; no *amour propre*
flows to limbs or face to inform her

with a self-energizing life.
But she now frees herself from the spot
where the two familiars sit hulked as mounds
of ash and circumnavigates the seastrand
of musical devotees, toeing close
enough to touch the tide, the wave of notes

busting from the band shell. And finding one
abandoned tattered sheet to claim as hers
she cautiously lets herself lie down, face up,
alone, a primal *I* among the razz.
At every reach, an instance and example
of consumerhood, the dreck and spillage

of the sacred—what makes it so?—
human heart. There's still time for her
to emerge, in the fluxion of the days,
an authority of her soul. Isn't there?
But isn't there the wish for fuel and spark,
the fury to live, a fundamental

idea and wake-up call, in each of every
one who showed up, potato salad or
cello in hand, to listen for the note?
Wouldn't that be a planet,
its reflected light furled around itself
in such a timid stance, amid the fireworks?

The New Age

"There's danger on the edge of town."
—Jim Morrison

1:   Sex Kitten

The power began in my cunt.
Base chakra, the worshipful
Had called it, but I knew better,
Never mind what I'd been told.
The difficulty was waiting
For the man I lived with to leave
The house. (On his way out I
Told him to smile.) Then I lay down
On the flowered rug,
Lifted my skirt
For the god to service me.
I tried to understand his hobbies,
I wet my fingers to put them
Where they might please him, but he
Snatched them up and pinned them
To my sides. When I came, the surge
Was without diminishment.
The electric serpent remembered
Its journey up the spine, reached
The doorknob at the top of the head,
Tried to open the door.

2: Attachments

I woke at three in the morning with the saffron monks.
"You will love me," we chanted to the gods.
"I will pick up the check," we chanted.

The eyes of the young guru and the old guru and the first,
Dead guru stared, fiery clocks, from the ashram's blue walls.
I stuttered as I read from their hymnal.

By six at night old trap doors gave way in my head.
I crashed to the floor of an underground warehouse,
Where my parents were taking turns sawing one another in half.

My father's hands were palsied. My mother's were skinned.
"Help out, here," they said.
"Don't be a drudge."

Above us the monks had risen from their pillows
And the flabbiest one was leading a dance.
Their incense smelled of lavender, and I was so happy

I sawed and sawed.

3: Burnt Orange Taxi

Everything mysterious begins with
A taxi. Mine was foreshadowed by
The color of a guru's robe: the interior
Of my taxi had to be burnt orange.
Plenty of suspect taxis cascaded
Down the broad avenue, plenty with their
Vacancy signs lit. I stood with my luggage
On the corner by the Port Authority
And repeated my prayer, the one for
A lively orange taxi. My arm,
I knew—though I couldn't guess how—would lift
On its own at the collision of right
Circumstances. The moment came, I hailed,
The driver stopped. The uphostered seats, the ceiling
And dashboard were more orange than a golden
Goblet. My driver's dashiki was more orange
Than a swami's middle eye. "Bronx, please," I said,
And he swiftly complied, without the usual
Angry expressions. "Ah, the provinces,"
He said. "That sure pushes my homesick button."
In the back seat I was barely there,
Nothing much my own was left in my head.
I was busy reconstructing the blue
Interior of an ashram. Clearly
My powers were on the rise.

4:   Blue Lights

Then one day the trees were blue lights.
So were the cars, so was I.
We pulsed obscenely, unwitting
Indigo dancers stripped to
Bare essence. I blinked. Nothing
Was solid. My hands were a mass
Of intertwining sapphires,
And the elderly couple
Strolling arm in arm was staring.
"Wonder what she dropped into
Her coffee," the lady muttered.
"Wiseass," said the man. But *they* pulsed
Bluer, a smoldering ultimate
Kind of blue, than anything.
I pretended I was
An experimental flash photographer
Snapping ultra-micro-organisms
No one ever sees. I would shoot
The final shot of earth before
It shattered into a zillion
Uncontrollable bombs, but by nightfall
I couldn't stand it anymore.
I curled up in the dirt
Of the quiet park, my eyes jammed shut.
If I wanted the true world
All I had to do was open them.

5: The Little Prophesies

That miserable bastard you slept with at seventeen?
He'll be buried under the rubble of a catastrophic earthquake.
(Three years later he move to California.)

Your humorless ninth-grade teacher, the one with frizzy hair
And stiff-tipped breasts? Hit on the head with a brick.
(No way to verify.) From the golden mind,

From the starkest chamber of truth, the prophesies
Stamped their little feet and I bid them surface.
It was June. The prevailing winds were from the tropics.

From the open windows I could hear Mrs. Cancino's
Blues piano strike its phatic refrain.
In the kitchen my boyfriend stood naked by the stove,

Stirring a pot of fish broth and egg whites.
I sat in the dining room nodding my head.
Five days since I'd eaten anything.

Silently I was asking,
What's my fate? as the moon led
Its fictional light across the sky.

6:   Rough Neighborhood

I opened my jaw and shoved my fist
Into my mouth. I held my breath
Until my ribs ached. I was crazy,
Or I was trying to understand the fear
Of death. In the mornings I had to pace;
Afternoons I had to lie on the mattress
To stare at the sun. One day I climbed,
Sweaty and half-dressed, onto the fire escape.
I heard gunshots and a whistling like missiles.
I smelled *pernil* being grilled on the roof.
A man in the alley carried a flag
Across his shoulder. Was it already
The Fourth of July? I threw my house keys
Down between the rust-eaten slats;
They made a sweet hammering sound against
The narrow steps. "Where do you live?"
Cried the man. He held up my keys.
In anger I bit down on the stone
Window ledge until my tongue bled. I bit down
On my hand like a lion carrying a cub
And crept back inside to safety.

Unfinished Music

1.

The perfect-postured, white-sleeved players
      inside the band shell are grinding out
            Vivaldi, Stravinsky, De Falla.
                  Frenetic arms flailing at all angles,

they're a swarm of mites eating the meat
      of a halved walnut. No lullabies this late-August night
            but Allegro, Vivace, Andante,
                Song of Love's Sorrow, Dance of Terror.

The concert-goers swat mosquitoes,
      and a hot jerky wind conducts more than a few
            early fallen leaves among the rows
                of slatted seats. In the second row

(for a seat here, you have to hurry,
      early in the day, be dying to see
            the exactitude of fingertips stretched
                to taut strings), an old woman's falling,

her head dropping into the lap
      of a teenaged girl. The girl laughs, sweetly nervous,
            tries to shift her bare shoulder, tilt and lift
                her pelvis from the seat—and the woman

shakes awake, astonished,
      then drops again.

2.

This morning I'm looking at my habit
      of collecting fragments: this shell,

why did I take it? From which sea?
Its outer spirals are missing and the center

of that home lies exposed. What in hell made me snap open
my half-used makeup case in the woods
and carefully place this half a butterfly,
this solo black and yellow wing?

And the owl's claw? From the white
and dirt-stiffened foot, its four talons
curve their death—as though they still could—
toward my open hand.

3.

The woman asleep at the concert
looks like Bette Davis in something I've seen,
handsomely over eighty. What does she want
in her pink-framed glasses, sleeveless blouse

and white shorts, pink earrings jangling
through shoulder-length waves? She's no fragment
or half-winged one, just a peculiar sleeper
who rushed, if not to hear the music

then to be near it, among us.
I want to ask how she keeps desire.
Frail, yes, but vigorous—look at her.
She's not exposed—why should she be—

on a strip of gutter, skin puffed and mottled
as red granite liquefied. Whatever she is,
lonely, old, *she's* not weeping
on a subway platform, barefoot,

a shoe in each outstretched hand. No not this woman
    but another had come to that, wind blasting
        through the sixth-floor windows, shards
            of liquor glass underfoot,

a woman barely recognized by
    herself. I'd wanted to ask someone
        how to keep desire—any desire—for life
            the night I forced my mother into a taxi

to the emergency room,
    where we waited, where there was not one
        psychiatric bed in the entire city,
            where the tired doctor told me, *she's fine.*

She's fine, you can take her home.

4.

It isn't a pristine glade
    that surrounds this lake, but Central Park;
        when I stop paddling, the boat pulls west to
            the brackish water by the shore. A lone figure

sleeps in a kiosk, his bundles around him.
    I take the oars again, tilt them till they lance
        the water's surface, and turn my rented boat
            back to the center of the lake.

I did not know, did not want to, I did not stop
    my mother's going by bus late January
        to the summer cabin, the small iron bed, electric
            switched off. Wrapped in frozen coats,

removing the bottle cap, swallowing
    —and her body not discovered till April,

a one-way ticket stub
in the pocket of her jeans.

From across the lake a loud splash:
two rough-clad boys prance on a ledge slanting
sharply to the water. One holds a rope
to a dripping mutt

crawling up from the lake. As it cowers
in exhaustion one boy lifts it
by the forelegs and tosses it in again.
No, no—not like that, not like that—

A man—their father?—steps from the trees
and kneels to retrieve it.
Nearby, a tuft of purple weeds waver
in the slow steady warmth. I rest my oars,

twist the cap off a jar of water, and drink.
A sudden swoosh—the tall weeds shudder and break—
a bittern, long-necked, iridescent,
points its beak and lifts across.

5.

I stand and walk from the concert into a quiet
unlit courtyard. In my mind a musician of silence sits
at a kind of piano. Each strike of the keys and a note
of silence is struck, with each chord more

silence—and something inside me calms
until I think each cry, moan, or laugh,
each scream and prayer is abated, annulled,
has never been.

But then she
    begins to talk to me: *No, not like that,*
        not like that. Not to want anything
            —even the torn and wounded things—

means not to exist. But stay here a minute
    where nothing exists, not even you.
        What if only you existed, you, the only part of me
            left? What could you do but want the world?

No, stay here, a minute—

Writer

Who doesn't speak, who carries in her grip
to the grave two knives? Let them drop and rust,
lay them to rest—or grip them yourself,

drag the blades across the poorly healed wound,
open up on 1963.
Mother is thirty, takes—for herself—a lease

on three rooms. (West Bronx; Shakespeare Avenue
no less.) Butterfly chairs, kidney table,
and iron lamps. Sofa bed. Writing desk.

I am five. She takes me once, caught too far
from home in the rain. What does she do
in these orderly rooms? A secret.

Months, she stays just months. Then returns to
Father and me with an inexplicable
fear of fire, inability to be alone.

She hoards, rounds the hated house with the crap
of one dispossessed, rotisseries and
box springs, electrical cords (unplugged), soiled

clothes and their hangers, great heaps of the un-
useable, unwearable, tide after tide
of soot and murk.... Some days the pots simmer

with ground beef sweetened with apples *Love is*
at the mercy and star anise. *of the elements*
Other days there's blood in fascinating

anarchy, a trail of it from room to room,
menses making its odd graffiti down
the pale freckles of her thighs and calves. *In 1958*

my psychiatrist (who'd been an obstetrician)
said women scream because they think they are
supposed to, said he could not stand to work

among screams Or she dresses for work
(welfare proponent, senior-center director,
nursery school sub) she likes but always

and quickly quits. *In 1958*
I was twenty-five, thought I had a great task
to perform. Then the baby began to cry

and I said to my husband, "I have to write,
get the baby out of here." I felt faint.
A stretcher, two men in the bedroom, ambulance.

In the hospital, voices from the next room:
"I can't sleep," they cry. Brightest elder
daughter of trash-poor Jews (who were rarely

gentle), my mother packs her closet with
suits she's given up, briefcase and notepads,
calendars, given up; and too the soft

sweaters whose pearl buttons slid, easy as breath,
in and out of the buttonholes. Given
up. By '88 when I visit I find

her in bed. *So rudely shorn of its dress*
that its gnarled angry roots wrinkle with wrath
The afternoon is warm, the mattress clumped

with covers. Mounded, utterly alone,
a refugee stricken in the hills.
She needs any other's breathing,

and so I lie next to her and we sleep.
Her depression—months and years—like the weight
of water falling on sodden ground.

Then she wakes and asks me—do I seem
to know how to get things done?—to help her
die. (Screw the doctors, she'd said, and their pills.)

    Kill me is what she says.

~

But this is no heroic life. And so
two years later we are crossing
the Whitestone, Father driving the turnpike

to Long Island. She curls up, fifty-seven,
in the back seat, head in my lap, matted
hair silver-streaked, mercurial rivers

running through Martian soil. Shadows
on the ceiling of the moving car:
trees and trucks, street lamps, familiar, broken-

down. *And soon the love is too much to be*
hidden beneath the ground. And too full to
be enclosed within the walls of the seed

He drives on in silence. Before the turnoff
for the hospital, I draw my fingers through
her hair, grasping at the roots. When I find her poems

and journals at the back of her closet
they are brittle, stuffed in a pillow case.
1951: I am eighteen, overcome

by a peculiar immobility,
home from work and school. I'm taken to see
a doctor, well-known, fancy, made to wait

in his waiting room. . . . Mother says he's arranged
EST, shock. He's never even seen me. . . .
The orderly daubs jelly in my mouth

without a word, every other week.
Another patient, middle-aged man,
trying to tell his wife their problems are not

only his fault. His slowness caused by
the repeated shocks. His wife turns her face
and does not listen. . . . Next visit, I arrive

at the clinic in my best suit, lipstick,
every hair in place, enter smiling.
The doctor is French; I entertain him

with my French. Impressed, he decides that I
may stop.
              I am numb, have stopped writing. . . .

A pillow case, which the daughter unzips,
thrusting hands in, extracting typescripts
and carbons, the crushed will.

~

I would not have it

otherwise; who knows if before the sun
had straddled the broad sky, if such a dream
had come, if you would still be you

or I be I.

1933–1992

The Reconciler

Ex-prisoner, weightless heart, brick
In the underground construction of the dead,
I give your miniature passengers a twirl,
I set your Ferris wheel down in the sand.

This was your toy, orange and blue,
From the thirties. Remember it?
The riders, safe even as they spin?
Look!—I whisper to be gentle—

An engineer fashioned it. Mother, open
Your two glass eyes and look
At the miracle of engineering!
"Very nice," you say.

"Now pour me some chocolate from the thermos."
O Mother, my first poor handsel,
I'm tired of looking after you,
My body stiff around you as scaffolding.

And sure, why should *you* care
About equilibrium when—now I'll say it—
You've killed yourself? Mad starveling,
You're barefoot on a frozen drift of sand

On this city beach you once took me to
While Father was at work.
The black ocean unravels its ancient reel.
Disaster, disaster, where

Are your shoes? Can I salvage them,
Give you back your solid ground? Too late:
The tide has sucked them out.
Shadows rise and collapse on the waves

—restless dolls, a passing double-decker
Bus filled with clowns. Let's play,
Mother. Let's play. Here are
Two fat policemen riding unicycles

Down the boardwalk. Murderer
Of your murderer, let's topple them in a heap.
"Such chaos!" let's murmur, let's laugh.
"Such chaos!"

Lucifer of the Mind

Half-angel without manners, brooding at
The turnstile, brushing scurf from your shoulders:
The headlines of depression stagger across
Your newsprint, flare like match tips at the strike
Of your thumb. Here where anxiety
Rents the tunnels for the night I see you
Fretting with your treasures, tightening the loop.
This dark station heats, sears: the working hour,
The dreaming hour, my hair, lashes, fingertips
Are burning. You will burn me down.

This day, from my rooftop, I saw you crest,
Red temper set to cooling across
The grain of the gentle sky I should have
Plucked you down from with steady-handed tongs.

Pibloktoq

"In a state of perfect nudity she walked the deck of the ship; then seeking still greater freedom, [she] jumped the rail, onto the frozen snow and ice.... Then there commenced a wonderful performance of mimicry in which every conceivable cry of local bird and mammal was reproduced."
   —ADMIRAL ROBERT E. PEARY, *The North Pole*, 1910, describing a case of *pibloktoq* (arctic hysteria) among the Eskimo

Its sufferers, it seems,
were women
—it being the norm
for a man to toss an

unsatisfactory wife
out into the snow. Sensible
choice, then, to perfect
the gesture of exposure

—as if madness might
become a figurehead
for a life, desired
as essential, as distinction

between oneself and
the brutality
of selves, a logical,
even reasonable,

severance
the weak self
could not otherwise
have made.

For a moment to compose
I, I, I

out of the sfumato
of days, a little brilliance,

a little madness
delivered like a fuel
to the blazing island.
                    As if the only other option

were the brain's captain
devising a full-blown
catatonia to scuttle
that *I*-boat, consciousness,

and drown.

Two

"He regards the history of his life before
...as an experience that had occurred
in the life of quite a different person....
The accident may be considered the boundary
line separating two distinct lives
of the same individual.... Two selves
seem to dwell within.... One seems to be
deadened, crushed in the accident,
and the other is a living self whose knowledge
and experience are but of yesterday."

—BORIS SIDIS, *The Psychology of Suggestion*, 1909

Ziusudra in Warsaw

**Ziusudra (Sumerian Noah) was granted immortality
but not the power to bestow it, and can only watch
over the millennia.**

He leans against the stone of an abandoned Parisian-style courtyard.
The sky darkens above broken gargoyles, smashed
Heads of state. The June air of 1944 is dry, unseasonably cold.
He strains his better eye and beckons a child,
A girl with the placid smile of an angel, to suffocate him.

Happy to oblige she binds him in long plastic sheets, humming
As she works. She's a tireless enthusiastic worker, one of the Nazis'
Gilded youth; when the old man's unruly hair refuses to stay bound
She stuffs his mouth with it as he watches, indifferent.
A young boy accompanies her. He's naked as a cherub,

Rudimentary wings protruding like insignia from his shoulders.
He decides—as if playing a game of eenie meenie,
Like a Himmler choosing to cauterize genitals today or next week—
Where in the underworld Ziusudra should go.

As the girl works she hums a war song, a tune any patriot would
        recognize.
Why won't Ziusudra tell her to stop? Rip the plastic from her hands?
The children sentence him to hell, which is modeled after the mind.

Of the sun in the underworld—barely discernible to our all but blind
        grandfather—

Ziusudra says that it shines, constantly silver, as from the bottom
    of a lake.
Otherwise, he says, nothing is different, nothing he's not used to.

Each time he arrives, his frayed pelts, his old wife, his thorns
From the plant of immortality await him.

Storm Windows: Broken Song

"Little Paris," it was named:
Warsaw before *der khurbn*, famed

for theater in *der mame-loshn*,
the mother tongue, where often

the young woman and her younger sisters
would go in '29, knowing it was riskier

after dark in the Jewish section
but loving the music so, and the passions

—as though each actor knew each girl's own
longings. How she loved those overblown

emotions, someone's lover always lost, swept away
—as she too longed to be—"Some day, some day,"

I imagine she'd whisper. But after the musicals
she went with her sisters back home to their familiar

sisterly spats: one had dyed her dark hair blonde
and stolen a boy from another, one forgot to mend

another's dress.... And in their home that November,
as at the start of every Warsaw winter,

it was their task to pack the windows with rags, fill a space,
about an inch, between each double pane, as though they'd erase

the dim city, the snow that fell in tatters,
the darkening rows of houses, feed buckets clattering

against horses' bridles. Now what mattered
took place inside the small apartment: their mother's

talk of leaving Poland—no hurry, but soon—
and a relative in Canada who might have room.

But this talk the woman remembers not
as well as how they fought

to fill those windows, she and her sisters,
their last Warsaw winter, that winter

she turned twenty and fell in love
(in '41 he was detained, eventually shot,

but death is not what she wants to tell me, not
what's vivid for her now). She makes her own plot:

See *this*, she says, *this*:
we were three young girls at our task,

to fill those storm windows—oh, and rivals
we were, even at that—it's a marvel

we ever finished before spring. Each one had to be best.
And how did we fill them? Can you guess?

We kept a bag of colored rags—red, gold,
blue, green scraps of aprons, socks, old

dresses, nightgowns, tablecloths, coats—and these we sent
sprinkling down between the panes, to the very top vent

of the windows, until they were stuffed with our
tatters, like a drift of colored snow packed in glass. This was our

show, to blot the dark city with color, like the flurry
of actors singing in the Yiddish theaters. "Why worry"

—they'd always sing something that went that way—
"when worrying won't, won't change anything." I wanted to stay

in Little Paris. I was in love. Then she changes her mind,
waves a hand across her face and stops speaking this kind

of memory, no not this kind; nor how, one February,
so many were fleeing, a mad flurry, like snow.

No, leave it buried.

The Living Man

Kind, educated, the man
she'd hoped to marry was dead
back in Warsaw—Resistance
or the camps: Who knew?

This man raged and cursed
like the rough farm-hand he'd been.

Her back to us,
Grandma tended the potatoes,
peeling and cubing.

At the table, Grandpa made me
taste his beer and mocked me when
I couldn't stomach the bitterness.

A wholesome womanly smell
rose, like something beyond possession,
from her soup.

Lithuanian runaway,
he sat over his winter's beef
in an undershirt thin as skimmed milk,
gray as marrow. He spat
at the newspaper, hemmed in
by all the women and Blacks
making news in 1969.

At dawn he rode the D line out
of the Bronx to Brighton and the small shop.
Forty years he'd cut mirrors,
plates of glass, setting some
in frames twice or more his height.

At eighteen I left home
to live in one dark room with a man.
Grandpa phoned there only once
before he died (his body slamming
to the floor between his and Grandma's
twin beds).

He's kind to you? he asked.
Educated?
Useless man, he said.

To My Mother's Parents

Which one of you
Counted down the minutes
—as I have counted down—
She stood, textbooks in hand,
Her life quietly flaring out
On Mapes Avenue in the Bronx?
Was this the afternoon she'd been warned
Away from college? No daughter
Of his—and that's all there were, two
Daughters—would ever go. I don't think
It was the money, I mean who paid the fee
As my mother lay down like Isaac
On some shrink's midtown couch
—but no great voice cried Harm Not
This Girl. And which of you played
Shamed bystander, rinsing
Barley beads, chopping up the parsley,
While my mother clawed and bit
Through rags
In the shock room?
Here I court that God
To make me tender, a cool breeze
Blown across the altar, the idiot flames
Extinguished. But who was it
Made her swear to keep silent
Even from my father
Any news of breakdown? so that when
I was born and it happened again
And she opened the window

—me prone and trusting in her arms—
To step across the sill,
Who was there to say it might
Have been different, at least this girl
Might have been spared?

Wildfire

Picture my aunt at the head of
Grandma's hospital bed.
They whisper, conspirators.
"Stomach cancer," Auntie nods

Toward the other patient in the room.
"Spreads like wildfire."
There's a strong smell from that other
Woman: urine, blood. Auntie says

She too could've had cancer
But it was fibroids, the best
Kind of tumor, benign.
Auntie's gray coat

Wraps her immense body
Like a carpet smothering flames.
Her hair's thin and patchy:
Who's been tearing it out?

Long ago she swept me up
And we danced around the foyer.
"I love you, a bushel and a peck,"
We sang. At the hem of her skirt

A line of dancers linked hands
And danced. Auntie's beautiful
As a red-giant sun, strong enough
To shove stout Grandma from her wheelchair

Onto the kitchen floor.
Break finger bones. A wrist.

These things happen more than once,
But they're friends.

Grandma slams the buzzer, demands more ice.
More napkins! A straw! Nurse!
Raise the bed! Grandma grabs the rail,
Turns toward my aunt....

I'll leave them there. They have
A private joke to share.

Cradle, Keel

H.G., 1909–1993

And now she's fallen asleep
in the crowd: her arms slacken at her sides,

her book drops to the floor
of the rocking train. She's just the newest

passenger, destination
different than the one intended. Once more

she finds herself buffeted
by younger sisters, The Stupid One and

The Bleached One, packing trunks
for the move to Chlodna Street, fighting

over blouses.... (How proud
the family was, to be the only

Jews in the new building!)
And here she is, a grandma again, huffing

up the stairs (the blue
cradle she carries is for me, for my doll).

And here, at her table,
she tells me she has cats in her head,

kats-in-kop, meaning
scatterbrained. And in this dream she will rip out

her daughter's red hair
for no reason: yes, reason: her father's

dead and she's lost,
the child too close at hand.... And in this

—no, let's not
go to this dream. And here is a private

dream no one is worthy enough to hear.
Now there is a bed

in Flushing General, two black rafts
fixed and contracted

in her eyes' white lakes. She dreams of the air
between two cities,

the powerless, powerful air, cloud-panicked,
mercurial,

above the water between Warsaw
and New York.

Kats-in-kop, what was the name of the ship?
Leviathan, The

Leviathan. *I was flying above my body*,
she says in her dream,

*I was born to Sarah and Morris, I
was twenty, sailing third-class*, she says

in her dream, *close to the keel, old people*
slept on valises, there were no windows,

she says in her dream, *there were seasick children,*
men laughing in foreign languages,

I myself was happy—

Three

"Some saw the spider, others did not,
   but they knew that it must be the tarantula.
   They ran out of the house into the street,
   to the market place, dancing in great excitement....
   Others would tear their clothes and show
   their nakedness, losing all sense of modesty,...
   Some called for swords and acted like fencers,
   others for whips and beat each other."

   —H. E. SIGERIST, *Civilization and Disease,* 1943,
   describing tarantism, the "dancing plague"

The Sirens

"Thus the ship sailed by in safety
and the Sirens committed suicide for vexation."
—ROBERT GRAVES, *The Greek Myths: 2*

After-hour madams of
schwarmerei blowing open
the latches, banging heavily
into the bedrooms of those asleep,

ears plugged with the world's generic
wax; belly dancers—their meadows
heaped with bone—grinding to the waves'
flamboyant tambour and zils;

mad ones, plucked bald by the Muses
Apollo had gentrified (he
led them in all the formal dances,
the phrase "Nothing in Excess"

always on his lips); nightclub
floozies the Muses challenged in song,
then—to demonstrate their perfect grace?—
mangled at the wings and stripped every

feather from for crowns; the Sirens,
bird-girls, singing *Come love us, come
love us,* girl-faced and deadly, chained
to the other side of anything that

passes for benign: comfort of old
age, steady rhythm, passion within
reason.
       Nothing licensed
but rage, they lived where the sea

is not unkind but opens her mouth,
white teeth chomping, where the rocks
catch their code word: *lure lure*.
They were girls who learned

to love that first whiff of honest brine
from ripped flesh,
slain men's bones hollowing,
fluting the wind. It was a world

of sacrifices, heroes or poor
dupes crunched between the jaws of
unwholesome semidemigods,
but what music! for which Odysseus,

who loved their wildling song, had himself
lashed to the mast and listened—from
the safety of his ship. One did not,
then or now, die for music. Passion

was to be found at home, faithfully
tied to her knotted loom. No Sirens
now, a choice Odysseus' poet
would have us understand: tsunamic

excess of beauty, inarticulate
consummation of the heart in one
fulgurant eros-storm

—or, reasonably,
life. The Sirens were done in
by the hero's firm hold

of his senses. Now reason's busy
producing monsters. Sanctioned
music. Art for the conglomerate.
Bored arousal at the whipping post.

The gentle silence of lethal
injection. Slurry marriages
and the smarmy reportage of
affairs. Worth dying for? Where

is the aching irresistible song,
that vilified music from
the madness realm? The safer we are
the more reasonable somehow that sound.

This City

I was about to say *If you've never*
lived in a city—but what I mean is
if you've never lived in *this* city.
I was born in this city and while I don't want
to talk about the Bronx or why I left it, I can tell you
a hundred Guatemalan sweaters tumbled from garbage bags
this morning on Eighty-fifth and Amsterdam:
fierce blues, purples thick as the pulp of grapes,
vibrant, almost violent, reds
slipping from the black-glossed bags.
They reminded me of exotic birds trying to lift
from oil-slick pools.
A man in a somber suit stood waiting for the bus,
and I imagined him headed uptown to a funeral.
But here he was, waylaid by cardigans,
a flock of wool sleeves, and his bus rerouted
for the street fair. I hoped he'd change his plans
and linger by the cactus stand
or the used-coat sellers, at a cookie-maker's or the vat
smelling thickly of grease and salty fries.
I wanted to stop,
skip whatever I'd been on my way to, not buy anything
but take it all in, the way last night the moon
was taken in through the canyon of each cross-street
in midtown. As I rode a late bus home
each street's separate moon dangled from a chain
of silver buildings. The bus went up Avenue of the Americas,
over to Broadway, past the Cineplex with pulsing marquee lights,
a billion syncopated bulbs orbiting
the names of stars. While my bus was stopped
I tried to focus on one bulb, an individual
with a destiny, its own on/off thing.

If it went out, the whole pattern
broken.

        Just now I'm listening
to a small crowd five years back and uptown
in the Bronx. An unlocked door, a kitchen
doused with gasoline, a struck match. Fire rising in V formation
from the third floor to 4, 5, 6. *6J—*
don't forget 6J. Pound the door, harder.
Are they home? Already gone?
It's three a.m.
Firehoses hiss and sink in the dreck
of our flooded lobby.
Mrs. Cancino's slippered feet are frozen and soaked.
Marsha keeps her bird's cage held high. *Yes*
there's a body in the alley. Someone jumped,
they won't let us see. Where's Mrs. Miller?
She needs her walker. Who struck the match? A jealous—who?
Before I let them go, should I say he's
elsewhere now, serving time
in a different story? Tonight he's still in this one
with the old woman on 5, both Martinez kids
who crawled under their bed, and the girl
who leapt in her multicolored robe, sleeves on fire,
and landed on her spine. I tell you
there's no room inside a person inside this city;
the way those lights race around the marquee
you can't see them as separate anymore.

Monster

Here in my colander, as I wash the ripe
strawberries I bought on Broadway,
is a green berry, a monster. It is entirely
green: the stem, leaves, the berry itself,
small and green. The seeds that coat it are slightly

darker than the green of the berry.
Looked at head-on it's a green sun
emitting green petal rays. And it's hard,
has the hardness of something born too soon,
something born dead and put in a jar.

What's frightening about this berry
is what frightened me about the baby
they passed around in ninth grade,
sealed like preserves in syrup:
how it looked at once alien and familiar,

how it almost looked like something you
might have held on to and called yours.
Once near Ninety-second Street
I saw a woman with a one-year-old
in her arm. The woman was swaying

as though she might faint, as though
she were a stick of margarine
melting in a pan. She smiled,
the way someone on heroin smiles before
they nod off—and she was nodding off—

but just before the child slipped like a carton of eggs,
she jerked awake.
In her other hand she held a cucumber,

its green peel shiny with wax, a few bites gone.
I saw her try to fit it in the baby's mouth

    but the baby patted it as if it were a doll
whose hair needed smoothing. The child looked happy,
as children look before they're old enough
to know anything's wrong, when a drugged mother
about to fall asleep in the middle of Broadway

    with you in her arms is *the* definition
of mother. What do they know?
If the sun is green, then it's green
and that's fine. If they're born dead and put in a jar,
clearly this is how life was meant to be.

Sister

My sister with ringlets and bruises,
Black little bird.
You came to live with my mom, dad, and me,
Our little white family.
Came with your brown bag allotment
Of panties, nighties, socks.
I won't ask what your mama did to you.
I'll put you to bed with a doll and a knife.
We'll watch dad toast mom with a scotch and a curse.
"Excellent home," said the caseworker's notes.
"Look after your sister," the parents advised.
"We're going out."
So I put you to sleep with a mouse and a timebomb.
I shoved you under the soapbubble water
And sent you to bed in the bright afternoon.
To the parents I said,
"I'm tired of watching Miss Blows-to-the-Head,
Little Baldspots." Little sister,
Petrified of splinters, of doctors with tweezers: Go.

The next home for you had
Thirteen more wards, all of them cruel
—or so I dreamt.
Goodbye, goodbye to the little-girl bird.

Innocent sister, wherever you are:
Are you living, are you living at all?

After the Sacrifice

The English verb *to die* is akin to the Old Irish *duine*, human being

And afterwards, the sea befriended us,
Gave away its fish. It drank its own
Deep cup and did not pour the fishers down
Its icy throat. It always went like this.
The architect of grasses raised our corn
To the stars, the three-headed dogs howled
At the watchmen but sent us no fevers.
A woman furious with death might lift
Her eyes at night: the sky would hurl no fires
At her breast but hold its meteors clenched
Within its fist. Always afterwards, and
Until the peace gave way, between the human
And her shadow a kind of truce was made.

The Bridge of Sighs

"The 16th-century *Ponte dei Sospiri* connects the ducal palace
with the Venetian prisons. Its chamber is divided lengthwise by partition
so that persons going and those coming will not meet."
—STURGIS' *Illustrated Dictionary of Architecture and Building*, 1901

Hanging vertically from the capstone
      above the twenty-odd-storied building,
our country's flag seems just the flag

for a prison: its rust-red bars and the narrow
      night-blue window that contains
the stars. In the jurors' waiting room

I'm looking out past the rain over to Franklin Street,
      where, on about the fourth floor,
a walkway covered by thick fish-tank glass

connects this courthouse to the prison.
      From time to time the glass-distorted
lawyers and prisoners appear, suspended

in watery limbo above Manhattan.
      Trapped in the jurors' room,
dozens of us, judged unfit to serve

because we were victims of crime,
      are returned here like repeat offenders
day after day for yet another judge to try us.

If by lunchtime I'm not picked
      I'll visit Trinity Church again.
Yesterday an organist was playing a fugue,

pipes bellowing fire and brimstone.
       Such a harsh resounding lesson
might have woken the dead

but the men and smattering of women
       asleep in the pews
held fast to their sleep.

One man pulled his soiled
       woolen cap down over his face
and shifted close to the wall.

I walked to the empty chancel, where I could turn
       and look up at the player,
wondering if he knew his "audience"

might be dying—or dead. He went on.
       They seemed to go on too,
despite the pipes' booms and heralds,

as though each sleeper were beyond
       ordinary range of earshot,
an isolated god

drifting in free-fall through a silent
       universe, sickly sleep
message enough

that he wanted to live.
       I remembered, the night I was held
against the stairwell,

how I prayed my silence
        would keep me alive.
I remembered thinking, calmly,

that the silver gun protruding
        from his jacket
might have been a spike,

like the ones that secured the criminal
        to his cross.
Maybe I pictured this because he

wore a cross around his neck,
        which he sucked on
as he told me what to do.

The bad dreams came later, the sweats,
        paranoia so fierce I couldn't look at a man
(even the one who lived with me)

without feeling my flesh tighten
        as if I were locked inside a cell.
If I could meet him again, if we could

redeem one another (*but its chamber divided*
        so that persons going and coming
will not meet) I'd tell him:

gods of division pace the bridge between our

actions and who we've forgotten
we are. On and on

they play ther irrelevant music
        while the boy you were burns
along with the rest of us.

Answer

The ocean opens its minatory door
    and suggests that the land, from South Carolina
    to New England, had best come inside.

A day after the hurricane
    this news photo appears: four swimmers
    struggling an unknown body ashore.

One man, eyes shut in effort, grips it
    from behind. A woman in mirrored sunglasses,
    big body heedless of its dainty bikini,

Hoists the limp right arm; another man tugs the left.
    Wading behind the heroes,
    one woman grabs her own hair

As if she'd tear it to the waves.
    But all's calm now; now the ocean lets them
    wade ashore with their fish-body prize

Which soon enough someone will claim,
    there will be flowers, the fuss
    over a grave. Lord gives,

Amen, Lord takes.
    But the drowned one?
    Bent at the knees, legs submerged,

Naked save for sheer white briefs:
     what could he want? His head bows
     toward its element, water,

In unspeakable—no, untranslatable—communion,
     chest collapsed, pressed into silence
     by the thumb of God.

Pelham Bay

"Fishing, with the arid plain behind me
Shall I at least set my lands in order?"
                    —T. S. ELIOT

Middleworld, ex-utopian haunt
of ooze and schist, *No-place* of cattails and clay fields
and marshland clam-gatherers who called this
haven *Aquegenum* (or so I read,

homesick as any primitivist for my
local lost paradise, on the wall map
in the Native museum), this place that is
always *Some-place* now, midsummer,

for a purple-suited water-skier's race
across the bay, motor blamming through the foam.
On the beach, not a stone's throw from home
(it's called *South* Bronx now, the City's backside),

the radio's the thing, discord of a thousand
jingles; and a thousand bodies baking
half-naked on the sand. Children greased in
coconut oil and floured with sand....

"You ain't shit, you ain't shit," a teen screams to
his younger resemblance. Further down the shore
one brave little girl lifts by its tail what's
left of a horseshoe crab, flips it over,

exposing the still innards. Is it something god-like
like forgiveness, or the mirroring
work a parent does, eye to eye with
her infant, that makes the filthy water

break its reverie and heave back on shore
our offerings: chicken bone, beer bottle,
tampon, rind? so that walking the packed beach
is like catching half a nap's worth of dreams,

dreams inhabited by oracles and louts,
crisp breaths of salt and the moodiness
of an unbathed latchkey child.
But to climb, late afternoon,

past the beach, beyond the snail-encrusted
jetties, up to the cliffs, near where the once-
forest (*still* forest) deciduously
begins, is to see the original cause:

urgent hunger and its satisfaction.
Here's a woman, coarse black hair tied back with
twine, gathering past-autumns' displaced leaves
in a smoky mound, poor fire crackling

upward like the mumblings of prayers.
She's calling to her son; he pretends not
to hear, tossing stones, targeting the shoals,
where the reef bell rings its plangency.

The father's fishing, or waiting for fish,
two rods buried deep in the spongy sand
and anchored by rock. He will not leave
until he gets what they came for, and so

he settles down, old legs dangling over
the cliff. He works at flattening his oily
hair with a half-toothed comb. In an hour,
another son, the elder, emerges

from a last swim, wringing out the edges
of his camouflage pants. He'll sit
beside the father now, still unfed,
the sky's red yolk dipping, gone. They listen

to the tide's ideas, prototypical
voice and steady heart—*nostrum innominate*—
down where the fishing lines go slack
and disappear.

Notes

"Chansons": The story of Inanna's descent to the underworld is translated in *Inanna: Queen of Heaven* by Diane Wolkstein and Samuel Noah Kramer (Harper & Row, 1983).

The descriptions of pibloktoq, by A. A. Brill and Admiral Robert E. Peary, were reprinted in *Mysteries of the Mind* by Robert M. Goldenson (Doubleday, 1973). "Peary found that attacks of this disorder...were not uncommon, and were confined almost wholly to women," writes Goldenson. "The basic reason why Eskimo women are subject to periods of brooding anxiety appears to be their inferior status in society."

"The Sirens": "Now reason's busy producing monsters" is a variation of Goya's "The sleep of reason produces monsters."

"This City" is dedicated to Suzanne Gardinier.

~

The word "ground-note" appears in Adrienne Rich's poem "Transcendental Etude" (*The Dream of a Common Language: Poems 1974-1977*, W. W. Norton, 1978):

> "...Everything else is too soon,
> too sudden, the wrenching apart, that woman's heartbeat
> heard ever after from a distance,
> the loss of that ground-note echoing
> whenever we are happy, or in despair."

About the Author

JANET KAPLAN was born in the Bronx; she attended Lehman College and Columbia University, and earned her MFA degree in poetry at Sarah Lawrence College. Her poems have appeared or are forthcoming in *The Paris Review, Ms., The Greensboro Review, Alaska Quarterly Review, Western Humanities Review, American Literary Review,* and the *Monitor Anthology of Magazine Verse & Yearbook of American Poetry,* among others. A limited-edition chapbook of her poetry, *The Solid Ground,* was published in September 1996 by the Premier Poets Chapbook series in Rhode Island. In 1991 she won the Bronx Council on the Arts' BRIO Award in Poetry. She teaches creative writing at Hofstra University.

Recent Titles from Alice James Books

CELIA GILBERT, *An Ark of Sorts*

B. H. FAIRCHILD, *The Art of the Lathe*

LISA SEWELL, *The Way Out*

SHARON KRAUS, *Generation*

ADRIENNE SU, *Middle Kingdom*

ELLEN DORÉ WATSON, *We Live in Bodies*

KINERETH GENSLER, *Journey Fruit*

CYNTHIA HUNTINGTON, *We Have Gone to the Beach*

NORA MITCHELL, *Proofreading the Histories*

TED DEPPE, *The Wanderer King*

ROBERT CORDING, *Heavy Grace*

FORREST HAMER, *Call & Response*

E. J. MILLER LAINO, *Girl Hurt*

DOUG ANDERSON, *The Moon Reflected Fire*

DEBORAH DeNICOLA, *Where Divinity Begins*

RICHARD McCANN, *Ghost Letters*

RITA GABIS, *The Wild Field*

SUZANNE MATSON, *Durable Goods*

DAVID WILLIAMS, *Traveling Mercies*

MARGARET LLOYD, *This Particular Earthly Scene*

TIMOTHY LIU, *Vox Angelica*

ALICE JONES, *The Knot*

JEAN VALENTINE, *The River at Wolf*

Alice James Books has been publishing poetry since 1973. One of the few presses in the country that is run collectively, the cooperative selects manuscripts for publication through competitions. New authors become active members of the press, participating in editorial and production activities. The press, which places an emphasis on publishing women poets, was named for Alice James, sister of William and Henry, whose gift for writing was ignored and whose fine journal did not appear in print until after her death.